Non-fiction Level 4

T0385963

Fantastic falcons

by **Kate Riddle**

PEARSON

Contents

Falcons are birds of **prey**. This means that they hunt other birds or animals for food. They are strong and can fly very fast. They are also very beautiful.

Hunting with birds of prey is called falconry. Falconry has been a tradition in the Gulf for thousands of years.

Long ago, falcons were trained by the Bedouin people to hunt and catch animals and birds. The birds and animals caught by falcons **provided** food for the Bedouin families and helped them to **survive** in the desert.

Falconry is still important today and is a popular activity in the Gulf.

A hood is placed over the head of the falcon when it is not hunting. This helps to keep the bird calm.

Hood

This is a stand for the bird to sit on when it is not training.

Perch

A person who trains a falcon to hunt is called a falconer. A falconer has special equipment for training falcons.

Glove

The glove protects the falconer's hands and arms from the bird's sharp claws.

Lure

These are thin straps tied onto the falcon's legs and held by the falconer.

Jesses

This is an object which is covered in feathers. The falconer swings the lure in the air. When the falcon lands on it, the bird is given food as a reward. This helps to train the falcon to come back to the lure after hunting.

It takes two to four weeks to train a falcon.
The falconer must keep the bird on his or her arm for
a few hours every day to help **tame** it.

7

Their eyes **magnify** what they see like a pair of **binoculars**! They can see things much sharper and clearer than humans.

They have strong legs.

They have narrow tails.

They have sharp, hooked claws which are also called 'talons'.

Their beaks are strong, sharp and hooked.

They have narrow and pointed wings which help them to fly very fast.

9

Falcons hunt mostly during the day. They usually hunt other birds but sometimes they eat small animals and **reptiles**.

Falcons can see so well that they can **spot** their prey from over a mile away!

Falcons hunt by diving through the air very fast. They catch their prey with their hooked claws and use their sharp beaks to eat it.

Falcons nest in high places such as mountains, tall trees and sometimes buildings. This is to make sure that their chicks are safe.

The chicks are white when they are born and grow their feathers in 3–5 weeks. They learn to fly at about 40 days. They **practise** by jumping around and testing their wings. The name for a baby bird learning to fly is a fledgling. The adult falcons look after their chicks until they are strong enough to look after themselves.

Falcons lay about 3–4 eggs and **incubation** takes about 29–32 days per egg. When the chicks **hatch** they are very hungry! The **female falcon** usually stays with her chicks while the **male falcon** hunts for food.

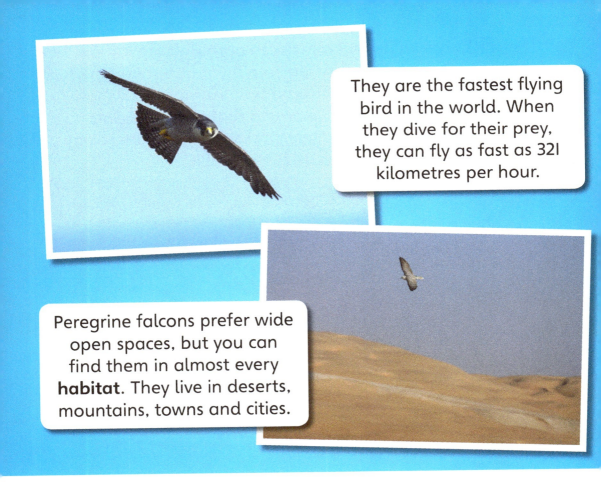

They are the fastest flying bird in the world. When they dive for their prey, they can fly as fast as 321 kilometres per hour.

Peregrine falcons prefer wide open spaces, but you can find them in almost every **habitat**. They live in deserts, mountains, towns and cities.

The peregrine is a popular breed of falcon in the Gulf. Read some facts about the peregrine!

Some live for up to 17 years.

A peregrine falcon calls out 'kak, kak, kak' when it is scared.

They have a **wingspan** of about 1 metre.

The word peregrine means 'to travel'. Peregrine falcons often **migrate** and travel long distances!

Did you know that peregrine falcons live on every
continent except Antarctica?